THIS BOOK BELONGS TO

_____

_____

A JARROLD COMPANION

# WORDS OF JOY

Surely the strange beauty of the world
must somewhere rest on pure joy.
LOUISE BOGAN

Let a joy keep you. Reach out your
hands and take it when it runs by.
CARL SANDBURG

A woman has a right to joy and pride and
contentment if her children have grown up
courteous and kind, honest and loving.
CHARLOTTE GRAY

The pleasure of life is according to the man that
lives it, and not according to the work or place.
RALPH WALDO EMERSON

## WORDS OF JOY

There is a joy in the possibilities of any actual life
and a deeper joy that comes with a sense of sharing
the whole and endless adventure of mankind.

IRWIN EDMAN

Certainly it is important to do
things that provide enjoyment.
But fun cannot be the end that shapes man's life.
If all is "enjoyed" one will not know true joy.

GEORGE W. MORGAN

Happy days are here again,
The skies are clear again,
Let us sing a song of cheer again,
Happy days are here again!

MUSICAL COMEDY,
*CHASING RAINBOWS*

## WORDS OF JOY

There are some people who have the quality
of richness and joy in them and they
communicate it to everything they touch.
…With such people it makes no difference
if they are rich or poor: they are really
always rich because they have such wealth
and vital power within them
and they give everything interest,
dignity, and a warm colour.

THOMAS WOLFE

What a fine lesson is conveyed to the mind –
to take no note of time but by its benefits,
to watch only for the smiles
and neglect the frowns of fate,
to compose our lives of bright and gentle movements,
turning always to the sunny side of things,
and letting the rest slip from our imaginations,
unheeded or forgotten.

WILLIAM HAZLITT

Each moment of joy we reach for strengthens
our spirits. Joyful memories can sustain
us through days of long hard work. Like rain, joy
comes and goes, yet its nourishment
keeps our spirits alive.

*TODAY'S GIFT*

'Tis easy enough to be pleasant
when life flows by with a whistle,
But the man worthwhile is the man with a smile
when he sits down on a thistle.

Accept the pain,
cherish the joys, resolve the regrets;
then can come the best of benedictions –
"If I had my life to live over, I'd do it all the same."

JOAN McINTOSH

## WORDS OF JOY

Joy appears now in little things.
The big themes remain tragic.
But a leaf fluttered in through the window
this morning, as if supported by the rays of the sun,
a bird settled on the fire escape, joy in the
taste of the coffee, joy accompanied me as
I walked to the press. The secret of joy
is the mastery of pain.

ANAIS NIN

Joy is what happens to us when we allow
ourselves to recognise how good things really are.

MARIANNE WILLIAMSON

Life is a sweet and joyful thing for one who has
some one to love and a pure conscience.

LEO TOLSTOY

## WORDS OF JOY

The house, the stars, the desert –
what gives them their beauty is
something that is invisible.

ANTOINE DE SAINT EXUPERY

A thing of beauty is a joy for ever:
Its loveliness increases; it will never
Pass into nothingness; but still will keep
A bower quiet for us, and a sleep
Full of sweet dreams, and health,
and quiet breathing.

JOHN KEATS

I love the modern mother
Who can share in all our joys,
And who understands the problems
Of her growing girls and boys.

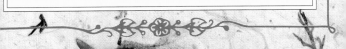

## WORDS OF JOY

*Why should we refuse the happiness
this hour gives us, because some other
hour might take it away?*
JOHN OLIVER HOBBS

*By being happy we sow anonymous benefits
upon the world.*
ROBERT LOUIS STEVENSON

*Harmony provides us with the inner peace
we need to appreciate the beauty that surrounds us
each day, and beauty opens us to joy.*

*I consider the world as made for me…
It is my maxim therefore to enjoy it while I can.*
TOBIAS GEORGE SMOLLETT

Whenever you are sincerely pleased,
you are nourished.
RALPH WALDO EMERSON

The man who gives pleasure is
as charitable as he who relieves suffering.
GEORGE MOORE

There are only three pleasures
in life pure and lasting,
and all are derived from inanimate things –
books, pictures, and the face of nature.
WILLIAM HAZLITT

People need joy quite as much as clothing.
Some of them need it far more.
MARGARET COLLIER GRAHAM

# WORDS OF JOY

I watch the clouds against the blue,
slowly moving with great purpose
across the skies. I lie on warm grass
seeing faces in these giants as they pass.
I reflect for a moment on the wonder
of nature as the sun warms me
and the joy of life fills my body.

D. ANTONY

I actually remember feeling delight, at two o'clock
in the morning, when the baby woke for his feed,
because I so longed to have another look at him.

MARGARET DRABBLE

My child…if you could only know how full
of love and joy my heart is whenever I think of you
and the person you have become.

DEANNA BEISSER

## WORDS OF JOY

I *finally figured out the only reason*
*to be alive is to enjoy it.*
RITA MAE BROWN

We *should publish our joys*
*and conceal our griefs.*

One *joy scatters a hundred griefs.*
CHINESE PROVERB

J*oys are not the property of the rich alone.*

I*f you have a contented mind,*
*you have enough to enjoy life with.*
PLAUTUS

WORDS OF JOY

**H**appiness is an inside job.

**S**uccess is getting what you want.
Happiness is liking what you get.
A FATHER'S BOOK OF WISDOM

**A** problem shared is a problem halved.
A joy that is shared is a joy that is doubled.

**P**leasure and action makes the hours seem short.
WILLIAM SHAKESPEARE

**C**ontentment furnishes constant joy.
To the contented even poverty is joy.

Joy seems to me a step beyond happiness –
happiness is a sort of atmosphere you can live
in sometimes when you're lucky. Joy is a light that
fills you with hope and faith and love.

ADELA ROGERS ST. JOHNS

If you ever find happiness by hunting
for it, you will find it, as the old woman
did her lost spectacles, safe on her
own nose all the time.

JOSH BILLINGS

We call "happiness" a certain set of
circumstances that makes joy possible.
But we call joy that state of mind and emotions
that needs nothing to feel happy.

ANDRE GIDE

WORDS OF JOY

*Good heavens, of what uncostly material
is our earthly happiness composed – if we only
knew it. What incomes have we not had from
a flower, and how unfailing are the
dividends of the seasons.*
JAMES RUSSELL LOWELL

*Who will tell whether one happy moment
of love or joy of breathing or walking on a
bright morning and smelling the fresh air,
is not worth all the suffering and effort
which life implies...*
ERICH FROMM

*Let us open our natures, throw wide
the doors of our hearts and let in the sunshine
of goodwill and kindness.*
O.S. MARSDEN

# WORDS OF JOY

A baby is a thing of beauty and a joy for ever.
MARK TWAIN

Without love and laughter there is no joy.
HORACE

If you wish to be happy, we'll tell you the way;
Don't live tomorrow till you've lived today.

The mere sense of living is joy enough.
EMILY DICKINSON

Whoever is happy will make others happy, too.
ANNE FRANK

Happiness grows at our own firesides,
*and is not picked in strangers' gardens.*
DOUGLAS JERROLD

Every joy is gain
*and gain is gain, however small.*
ROBERT BROWNING

The more joy we have,
*the more nearly perfect we are.*
BENEDICT DE SPINOZA · *ETHICS*

There's not a minute of our lives
*should stretch without some pleasure.*
WILLIAM SHAKESPEARE
*ANTONY AND CLEOPATRA*

My life has been a tapestry
of rich and royal hue,
An everlasting vision of the everchanging view.
A wondrous woven magic in bits of blue and gold,
A tapestry to feel and see, impossible to hold.

CAROLE KING

There is no beautifier of complexion
or form of behavior,
like the wish to scatter joy…

RALPH WALDO EMERSON

Yes, in the poor man's garden grow
Far more than herbs and flowers –
Kind thoughts, contentment, peace of mind,
And joy for weary hours.

MARY HOWITT

WORDS OF JOY

$T$he laughter of man is the contentment of God.
JOHN WEISS

$I$ wish you all the joy that you can wish.
WILLIAM SHAKESPEARE

$J$oy is a net of love by which you can catch souls.
MOTHER TERESA

$T$aking joy in life is a woman's best cosmetic.
ROSALIND RUSSELL

$L$earn while you're young…there is much to enjoy.
GEORGE ARNOLD

## WORDS OF JOY

**H**ow do I achieve joy? I open my mind to it,
I look for it, and when I find it I let it flow
through my body. Joy always comes from within
then radiates out like a beacon.

VIOLET PATIENCE

**H**ow good is man's life,
the mere living! how fit to employ
All the heart and the soul and the senses,
for ever in joy!

ROBERT BROWNING

**Y**ear by year the complexities of this spinning
world grow more bewildering and so each year
we need all the more to seek peace and comfort
in the joyful simplicities.

*WOMAN'S HOME COMPANION*

*DECEMBER 1935*

## WORDS OF JOY

Do a little kindness,
Any sort will do;
Sure as life's worth living
It comes back to you,
Warms your heart and makes you
Happy as can be;
If you don't believe it,
Just try and see!

A happy life must be to a great extent
a quiet life, for it is only in an atmosphere
of quiet that true joy can live.
BERTRAND RUSSELL

The foolish man seeks happiness in the distance;
The wise grows it under his feet.
JAMES OPPENHEIM

## WORDS OF JOY

The good, as I conceive it, is happiness,
happiness for each man after his own heart,
and for each hour according to its inspiration.
GEORGE SANTAYANA

Laughter's joy celebrates
the moment we are living right now.
It is a gift we must share, or it will wither and die.
Shared, it grows and thrives, and always
returns to us when we need it most.

Whatever hour God has blessed you with,
take it with grateful hand, nor postpone your
joys from year to year, so that, in whatever
place you have been, you may say you
have lived happily.
HORACE

WORDS OF JOY

The rule of my life is to make business a pleasure,
and pleasure my business.
AARON BURR

Of all the joys that lighten suffering earth,
what joy is welcomed like a new-born child?
CAROLINE NORTON

Not what we have but what we enjoy
constitutes our abundance.
J. PETIT-SENN

What a wonderful life I've had!
I only wish I'd realised it sooner.
COLETTE

# WORDS OF JOY

The unconditional love a child can give,
to feel tiny arms around your neck
and hear the words "I love you" brings joy
that can never be forgotten.
JANE ACHILLES

There are two things to aim at in life:
first, to get what you want; and after that to enjoy it.
Only the wisest of mankind achieve the second.
LOGAN PEARSALL SMITH

Before he closed his eyes, he let them wander
round his old room...familiar and friendly
things...which were so glad to seem him again
and could always be counted on for the same
simple welcome.
KENNETH GRAHAME

## WORDS OF JOY

*The boy and girl going hand in hand*
*through a meadow;*
*the mother washing her baby;*
*the sweet simple things in life.*
*We have almost lost track of them.*
EDWARD STEICHEN

*The man who thoroughly enjoys*
*what he reads or does, or even what he says,*
*or simply what he dreams or imagines,*
*profits to the full.*
HENRY MILLER

*The whole life of man is but a point of time;*
*let us enjoy it, therefore, while it lasts,*
*and not spend it to no purpose.*
PLUTARCH

The test of an enjoyment is the remembrance
which it leaves behind.

J.P. RICHTER

Gladness of the heart is the life of man, and
the joyfulness of a man prolongeth his days.

APOCRYPHA

We find delight in the beauty and happiness of
children that makes the heart too big for the body.

RALPH WALDO EMERSON

A man should always consider how much he has
more than he wants, and how much more unhappy
he might be than he really is.

JOSEPH ADDISON

ALSO IN THIS SERIES

*Words of Comfort*
*Words of Friendship*
*Words of Love*

First Published in Great Britain in 1997 by
JARROLD PUBLISHING LTD
Whitefriars, Norwich NR3 1TR

Developed and Produced by
FOUR SEASONS PUBLISHING LTD
1 Durrington Avenue, London SW20 8NT

Text research by *Pauline Barrett*
Designed by *Judith Pedersen*
Picture research by *Vanessa Fletcher*
Printed in Dubai

Copyright © 1997 Four Seasons Publishing Ltd

All rights reserved.

ISBN 0 7117 0965 3

ACKNOWLEDGEMENTS

Four Seasons Publishing Ltd would like to thank all those
who kindly gave permission to reproduce the words and visual
material in this book; copyright holders have been identified
where possible and we apologise for any inadvertant omissions.

Front Cover: THE SEE-SAW, *Giovanni Battista Torriglia* b.1858
Fine Art Photographic Library
Title Page and Back Cover: COUNTESS OF VILCHES,
*Frederico de Madrazo* 1815-94
e.t. archive